# *Brighton's*
# SEASIDE STORIES

## A People's History

Published by QueenSpark Books, a charity and not-for-profit company which, for 45 years, has helped the people of Brighton & Hove to tell their stories.

www.queensparkbooks.org.uk

www.photosbrightonandhove.org.uk

Charity number 1172938

Company number 02404473


ISBN 978-0-904733-21-1

A catalogue record of this book is available from the British Library

Printed by One Digital, Woodingdean

Designed by Stella Cardus, Desktop Display, Brighton

Cover photograph courtesy of Royal Pavilion & Museums, Brighton & Hove


All details, dates and accounts in this book are taken from the original books and photographic website, and recent contributions. All efforts have been made to contact those whose photographs are featured. Please contact QueenSpark if you would like to update any information for future editions, and we will be happy to do so.

# CONTENTS

# Introduction

QueenSpark Books, for 45 years now, has been enabling the people of Brighton and Hove to tell their stories. Originally part of a network of community publishers and shops - and, sadly, the only surviving member since Centerprise in Hackney closed last year - we have continued to value, and publish, the 'lesser-heard' voices of our city.

Our books encompass tales of early-and mid-20th century hardship, working lives on the railways, bakeries, fishing, and the West Pier. Homeless and ex-homeless people have told their stories alongside LGBTQ individuals and recently-arrived Sudanese, Bangladeshi and refugee communities. Most recently, we developed a new approach to engaging young people with reading, writing, art and local history, through *Brighton's Graphic War*.

All of these stories constitute a unique archive, unlike any anywhere else - the hundreds of individual accounts paint a picture of a changing city as told by the people who live(d) here. However, due to the short print runs forced by financial necessity on publishers like QueenSpark, many of our books, particularly the earlier titles, are out of print. This means that, barring visits to archives such as The Keep (www.thekeep.info) or searching our old website for text snippets (http://archive.queensparkbooks.org.uk), most people do not have access to the stories.

Whilst it is impossible – for technical as well as financial reasons – to reprint all of our books, we are able to select 'the best bits'; to this end we brought together a team of volunteers to scour through our books and see what themes emerged.

Brighton and Hove being by the sea, it is no surprise that 'seaside' became a particular focus (although other themes such as 'work', 'leisure', 'shops' and 'entertainment' have also reared their head, and we hope to bring you these compilations over the next few years), and once we alighted on it we had no trouble finding all sorts of 'lost' material in our archive; this has been enhanced by some more recent contributions, and selections from our photographic website, www.photosbrightonandhove.org.uk.

Selecting the 'best bits' is by nature a highly selective and subjective judgement, but we hope that these stories interest you, as they did us. They describe how our seaside has been a different place for different folk, but has always been a central part of our city's history.

# Foreword

This people's history explains and exposes seaside Brighton and Hove in a way that formal reports and most history books can never do. The book is made up of rich and varied stories of individuals and their communities. The stories are at times heart warming, celebratory and joyful, sometimes they are mundane tales of poverty and hardship and on other occasions they are defined by sadness and tragedy.

There are accounts of people grappling with seaside nature, explaining their families and communities, resisting repression, asserting their sexuality, and exploring the possibilities of freedom. Stretching back from the present day to more than a century ago, we learn how the seaside worked and changed - including the beach, the piers, the entertainments, the fishing boats, and the catching of fish. We learn how national and international events intruded on the business of seaside fun: Brighton's seafront was indeed on the front line during times of war.

Reading this book made me think afresh about Brighton and Hove's seaside both in the past and today and, indeed, about the seaside more generally.

Beginning with the first recorded pleasure-seeking visitors in 1736, Brighton emerged as the modern world's first and greatest seaside resort. It was the trendsetter, producing the standards that other resorts - in Britain and across the seas - copied. The very essence of Brighton, its defining characteristic, is that it is seaside. It is beside the sea.

*Promenading along the seafront by the West Pier in the 1890s*

The long and narrow zone that separates the town (nowadays the city) and the inland from the sea is the seafront, which includes the all-important beach, of course. But the southern boundary changes according to the state of the tide: at extreme low tides we can walk on sand toward the extremities of the piers. The northern inland boundary is also indistinct but the fuzzy border is partly defined by the Regency architecture, the grand open spaces of parks and gardens and all-important minutiae of seafront railings, lamps and shelters.

Today the seafront is the major attraction drawing visitors to the city and also Brighton and Hove's largest entertainment venue. But what, exactly, is the seafront the front of? Is it the land or the sea? Is it society or is it nature?

Our seafront – and all seafronts - is a marginal zone between land and sea. It is an edge, a boundary, between two distinct and contrasting environments. It's ever changing: from hour to hour, seasonally and over much longer periods of time. The iconic seafront shelters that nowadays provide places for families to eat fish and chips, lovers to love and the homeless to sleep were originally designed for respectable Victorian holidaymakers to meet each other and keep out of the sun.

The seafront is a largely free space, although there have always been tensions between the freedom and pleasures it offers and attempts at regulation and constraint. The seafront is a place of display and exposure. Normal conventions and rules don't always apply: the naturist beach and Dukes Mound are classic examples.

The seaside assails our senses: apart from the sights and the views, it is a place with distinctive (and changing) smells, tastes, feel and sounds. It's a place where we use nature. Holidaymakers may sit and gaze, sunbathe or swim in the sea.

Apart from being a place of pleasure and leisure the beach was also a place of work, sometimes very skilled, hard and dangerous work. Brighton's ancient fishing industry went hand-in-hand with a rich fishing community. Although it has gone from the beach, the fishing industry continues today, working out of the Marina and Shoreham Harbour. Historically many fishing people were also involved in the business of entertaining visitors, for example taking them for pleasure trips on the sea, while at the same time, of course, extracting money from them.

This book, as a people's history, provides wonderful insights into how Brighton and Hove's seaside became an iconic and symbolic place: of freedom and leisure, of work and struggle, of encounters with nature, of passion and argument, of Brighton and Hove more generally as a place to be, of the very idea of the seaside and, indeed, of Britain. The people telling their own stories also helped make the seaside.

*Fred Gray*
*Emeritus Professor of Continuing Education at the University of Sussex*

**MY WAGES WERE FIVE SHILLINGS A WEEK** with the working week consisting of six days, although a couple of years later shops decided to close one afternoon a week and we chose to have early closing on Thursday afternoons. I remember spending many of my half days accompanying my Auntie Mabel to the band concerts on the Palace Pier when weather permitted. These expeditions were the highlight of my week for we used to hire a deckchair, buy a cup of tea, and spend about three hours enjoying the music.

Unfortunately this came to an end later in the [First World] War when the pier and the seafront became off-bounds and guns were positioned on the seafront in preparation for any likely invasion by the Germans.

*Lillie Morgan* At The Pawnbrokers

*A crowded fishmarket on the lower esplanade in the 1890s*

When not at school, I was nearly always on the beach, watching the fish being auctioned at the fish market or helping to pull the Luggers or fishing boats up the beach, while the fishermen put ice into boxes for the fish waiting to be sent away.

One day on the beach, near the Metropole, some youth about 15 got into difficulties in the sea, about 200 yards out, and started to scream and shout, going under. A crowd of people, including some soldiers gathered round and just stood watching. The youth was now crying feebly and although I was only 9, I was going to go in after him. Just then an old man, he must have been over sixty, in a blue serge suit, went into the water and using the breast stroke (I can still see it now) swam out to the youth, and, as he was going down again, grabbed him and started swimming back towards shore. About 20 or 30 yards out, the youth started struggling with the old man and started pulling him under. The old man started shouting "he's drowning me", but still kept trying to reach the shore with the youth. About 10 yards out, some of the soldiers and civvies went into the sea, and helped them reach the beach. The youth was saved, and the old bloke collapsed with exhaustion. The youth recovered and I remember him, tears pouring down his face, thanking the old man for saving his life.

A lady standing by organized a collection among the few people standing there and herself put a £1 note in. She said to him, "You're a very brave man". The old man thanked her, and, now shivering, (it was late summer) with his clothes still streaming with sea water, walked up the beach towards the promenade. I have seen some deeds and experiences in my time, but that was the bravest, greatest thing I ever saw.

*Bert Healey* Hard Times and Easy Terms

My mother had several businesses- one up in Southover Street, she had one up in Portslade, and one in North Road, Brighton at different times. Then she had a stall on the seafront. She gave up the stall in 1914... She didn't do bad, but war broke out in 1914. The day war was declared the beach was packed - then they all cleared off. She packed up after that.

*Mrs Wheatley* Shops Book

The time was now Autumn 1916. The Front was packed with soldiers in Khaki, and 'the Blues', the wounded. The Volks Electric Railway started from Palace Pier in those days, and I can always remember a doll dressed as a Red Cross nurse which was fixed to a collecting box for the wounded, outside the pay kiosk.

*Bert Healey*

In those days you were not allowed to undress on the beach and nobody, not even men, were permitted to go topless. All swimming costumes had little skirts which provided a straight line at the bottom by covering, however slightly, the thighs.

*Children paddling in the sea in the 1890s*

*Bathing machines on the beach in the 1880s*

Because of the regulations, you either had to undress in one of the bathing huts provided or bring your own canvas tent. The beach we always used was the one between the two groynes to the west of the West Pier. It was known as Jim Hatton's beach because he had the contract for the bathing huts on that beach.

*Len Goldman* Oh What a Lovely Shore (Brighton in the Twenties Through the Eyes of a Schoolboy)

In the early twenties, bath chairs with attendants could be hired near the Aquarium clock. 'Invalids' were sat in the chairs, blankets were wrapped around, the hood was raised if the weather was inclement, and with the attendant pulling the handle, and devoted relatives assisting from the rear, the procession would move up the slope of Marine Parade. They would pass shoe-shine boys with their footstalls advertising Kiwi, Cherry Blossom or Nugget [shoe polish] and the Brighton fishermen leaning against the esplanade railings - always dressed in blue jerseys, with weatherbeaten faces, they were conspicuous figures. Solitary people, their pale blue eyes scanned the distant horizons as though a second Marie Celeste was expected to appear.

They would probably have seen the paddle steamers Devonia and Waverley casting off from the Palace Pier. On these two well-known craft, a pleasant voyage to Ryde and back could be enjoyed for an outlay of five shillings. The good sailors feeling confident of keeping well during a return cross-channel trip to Boulogne spent 14s.6d.

*Harold Dawes* East Brighton in the Twenties (unpublished)

The seafront had plenty of attractions. There were bands that played on the Pier, two concert Parties, the one near Black Rock was called Jack Shepherd's Entertainers, the one near the West Pier was Ellson's Entertainers. At this one, talent contests were held on Saturday afternoons, but one was only eligible to compete if one had a paid seat. The cheapest was 6d.

I had earned 5d. that morning, and after a lot of persuasion my sister Emily gave me the other 1d. if I would sing her favourite song at that moment: "God send you back to me". She had been friendly with a South African wounded soldier, and he had gone home. So we walked there and back but happy because I won a Teddy Bear for first prize.

When I told Mum she said it was given me out of sympathy because I went in my weekday clothes. She said I looked like a "Sal Hatch", whoever she might be, but I was quite pleased, and entered again at a later date. I only got third prize, which looked like a tin bucket of pebbles. They were humbugs, but a bit disappointing as there was only a layer on top, the rest was paper.

*Daisy Noakes* The Town Beehive

One of the times we were all together was Armistice Day of the First World War. With young George in the pram, we all walked to Brighton Sea Front and along to the West Pier. Everyone seemed to be singing and dancing, and I remember soldiers and sailors in uniform, the worse for drink, staggering around.

*Daisy Noakes*

The beach below Banjo Groyne was extremely popular in summer, as it was sheltered from the south-westerly winds. In the thirties, arc lights were suspended from the railway supports, and other vantage points. Those interested indulged in midnight bathing, and this stretch of shingle and sand became known as the Lido beach. During the Second World War the beaches were closed for five years and thousands of tons of shingle accumulated here covering the access steps, the wooden supports and probably the flood lights. Now the beaches are all the same general level, and the men and boys who looked over the Banjo Groyne to admire the bathing belles below are no more to be seen.

Close by, Jack Shepherd and his troupe entertained holiday makers every summer with his shows. A small enclosed area facing the roadway contained a covered stage and some ten rows of deck-chairs for the paying audience. Passers-by could also see the acts for no payment, although an actor not required for a particular sketch would occasionally move among the crowd with the collecting box. His appearance with his face still covered with grease paint signalled a noticeable thinning out of the onlookers.

*Harold Dawes*

I have walked the promenade in all the seasons and in all weathers. On Easter Sunday, when the sun was shining on the thronging crowds, I got a tremendous feeling that it was all there for my entertainment. The young men in their enormously wide Oxford Bags, some with bow ties and often wearing blue blazers,

*The seafront on a windy day in the 1890s*

were shod in brogues...no adult wore shorts, at least not until the early thirties. Plus-fours were worn along the promenade as well as on the golf course. The young women, usually in groups, wore short, knee-length dresses and skirts, with flowered designs on silky materials. And those high heels!...

The clamour of the whole multitude, the mixture of local inhabitants and visitors of all types, stepping out, looking for amusement, flirting, whistling or humming the latest tunes, swinging their arms or walking arm-in-arm, smoking – especially cigars or pipes – talking loudly and without inhibition, the smiling faces, people in various stages of inebriation, dogs tugging at their leashes and dog-owners tugging at dogs, it all brought vividly to mind the old cliché: All human life is there.

*Len Goldman*

The beaches were crowded. A few old, wheeled bathing machines were there, others in existence had been relegated to an odd spot on the road near the bottom of Duke's Mound. The third beach east of the pier was known as Hatton's and on it were rows of changing huts for bathers. Volks Electric Railway, which carried over a million passengers in 1928, was guarded at each crossing point by a man, probably retired, who held a canvas barrier across as the rail car approached. He stood on the pavement side and warned anyone he saw leaving the beach. Casualties were few, just the odd dog which crossed at an unauthorised point and touched the live rail, causing him to emit agonising howls as he disappeared.

Near the half-way station, the line crossed the Banjo Groyne, and as the beach to the east was about 20 feet below the level of the groyne, the track crossed on wooden supports to the next groyne. At high tide these supports were partly covered by the sea, so the posters read " the railway above the sea".

*Harold Dawes*

*Early twentieth century street entertainment*

Black minstrels played their banjos at low tide on the sands, and would get the children to join in the choruses, I remember "Oh Moana" and the actions.

People on the Pier would throw pennies down to the sands, and the boys would scramble for them. All sorts of vendors were on the beach with newspapers, Brighton Rock and the Whelk Stalls where one could buy a small plate of whelks, cockles, mussels or winkles, and one could leave the plate on the beach to be collected.

*Daisy Noakes*

There was [also] Archie, the handless artist, who operated some little distance from the steps that came down from the west side of the West Pier. Born with stumps instead of hands, he covered them with little mittens, grasped a special pen between them and did portraits and silhouettes. And very good they were too.

*Len Goldman*

Between Palace Pier and Black Rock was to be seen the sand artist, who had his square of sand on the beach but near enough for the promenaders to view his work. On this large square of sand he would scratch likenesses of England's stately homes, and in relief he would do a very realistic wounded soldier lying down.

Each day he would renew it. Then sit with his cap waiting for an appreciative passer-by to give him money. He had his own rhyme in the sand which read: "Some carve their name in stone, I carve mine in sand, and I hope to carve my dinner with the aid of a generous hand".

*Daisy Noakes*

The West Pier was our nearest and the one I most frequently visited - you entered through a turnstile from the promenade, and started to wend your way seawards, past people sunning themselves on the deckchairs on either side of the windowed partition which ran for some 50 yards along the middle of the pier. You then approached the buildings, which formed the first bulge in the long straight profile of the pier.

This was the dance-hall and, behind it, the theatre. Having skirted this obstacle, you passed by a number of stalls of various kinds. Beyond this again there were shops selling sweets, photographic equipment, ices and so on. Behind these were the open -air stage where pierrots used to perform during the season.

Not far from the back of this stage was the great diving pool at the pierhead. This was used exclusively by a strapping amazon of a woman who, twice daily during the season, paraded around the pool area with a megaphone shouting 'Any more for the diving at the bay at the end of the pier?'. She wore a bathing gown over her tightly-fitting but decent swimming costume and really looked the part...She mounted an enormous diving structure of Olympic height, removed her gown, took up the megaphone again and began her spiel. This consisted of descriptions of the dive she was about to perform and was always spliced with wit. The great height gave her more time for her mid-air athletics: jackknives, somersaults, the lot.

She also told the audience that drowned women came up with their faces turned upwards whilst men came up with their faces turned downwards because, as she explained, they were ashamed to show their faces!

*Len Goldman*

Plenty of deck chairs for 2d. but one could sit on a wooden seat which sat five persons for 1d. each. This was painted on the back of the seat for one to read. And on Dalton's Beach kites would be flying, their strings attached to one of these seats.

*Daisy Noakes*

I first started as a page boy in 1922 at the Bedford Hotel. I stayed three years and then went to Grand Metropole as commis waiter. Went to the Sussex yacht club from 1927 to 1930 as steward. From 1930 I went out as a street trader.

The police were problems [for the barrow boys]. We used to work Gardner Street, we were allowed five minutes to put our barrow down, then move again. If not we got fined. 'Course, the police were very good then and the fines were a matter of about 10s. in them days; we got a living. Especially from the basket pitches on the beach. You had to get up at half past three and get a pitch for yourself, otherwise you didn't get one. They were fighting for them.

*Mr Winton* Shops Book

In the twenties Black Rock was a quiet spot, popular with those who were interested in the variety of marine life left in the pools among the rocks when the tide ebbed. The cliffs were not protected from erosion and falls of chalk were frequent.

Looking up to the top of the cliffs, a few buildings, including the Abergavenny Arms, could be seen on the edge or dangerously near it. A person walking eastwards along the esplanade near Arundel Road and desiring a stroll along the cliffs found this row of buildings preventing access. If a fairly long diversion wished to be avoided, there was an alternative route through a sweet shop to the back door, the grateful customer usually making a purchase.

*Harold Dawes*

The area above the beach was just a rubbly wasteland when we first started going down there. Sometime in the mid-twenties, the powers that be decided to develop this area. It stretched from the Fisherman's Hard to the east, right up to the Hove

*A family group on the beach in the 1920s*

*The paddling pool in the 1930s*

David Sewell

border in the west. As the work progressed many and wild were the speculations as to what was being built.

In the end, there was a children's paddling pool, the other side of the pier. On our side there was a boating pool, with rowing boats, paddle boats and motor boats. Further on, were the sunken gardens and the bandstand where military bands played on Sundays. There was great excitement at all these changes.

*Len Goldman*

The horse drawn cabs could still be seen in Marine Parade, but their numbers were dwindling fast as they gave way to the motor taxis, and even an unusual motor cycle combination with a large side-car designed for carrying paying occupants. Among the privately owned cars could be seen Studebakers, Crossleys, Calcotts, Overlands, Beams, Swifts, Lagondas., and even the humble Trojans and three wheeled Morgans.

Peace was broken by noisy motor-cycles bearing the names Douglas, Excelsior, Royal Enfield, B.S.A., Matchless and A.J.S. Speeding was discouraged, heavy cars were limited to 12 m.p.h. and penalties meted out to those apprehended ranged between fines of one or two pounds with alternative prison sentences of about fourteen days.

*Harold Dawes*

In the 20s, when my brother George was a choirboy, the Christmas treat included tea at the creamery in Pavilion Buildings. Ten years later we didn't get the tea but were taken to the pantomime at the end of the Palace Pier. In those days they were traditional, sticking pretty closely to the story line, and very great fun. The dames were delightfully vulgar but nice, and somehow respectable. There was no sleaze.

*Maurice Packham* The Church Round the Corner

*Digging for lugworms by the Palace Pier in 1927*

When we had a little money, we would buy a hand fishing line plus some lugworm bait from Sid & Dons, the local angling shop, then head off to the Banjo Groyne and a little fishing, much to the annoyance of the serious, older fishermen, who we would tangle lines with. The law of averages should have provided one fish, but we never caught a thing.

After a time, we would pack up and wander into Aladdin's Caves, an amusement arcade under the promenade by the Palace Pier, hoping to find a slot machine where somebody had not pressed the reject button to get their money back if it failed to work. Then on to the fish market to watch the local fisherman sell off his catch. Sometimes we would see a crowd of poorly dressed barefoot kids singing, dancing and beating a tin can drum on the lower promenade, being thrown coppers by people on the upper pavement level.

*Dave Huggins* A Pen for All Seasons

We crossed the Aquarium Terrace and reached the Aladdin's Cave by the Palace Pier. This was a subterranean funfair under the pavement itself, with slot machines, mirror maze and other attractions. 'Do here what you wouldn't do at home' invited the notice over the crockery smashing stall. You shied wooden balls at the plates on the shelves, a good way, presumably of getting rid of pent-up frustration. The proprietor of the stall was quite canny: he delayed replacing the crockery until the last fragment had been smashed. Where did he buy the replacements, I wonder?

I was most fascinated by the piano and violin machine. Instead of a bow, little rollers pressed over the strings while hammers struck away lustily behind. It was an ingenious piece of mechanism, certainly worth a penny a go. The last I saw of it was during the last war when rolls of barbed wire kept the public and, supposedly, the Germans off the front. The Aladdin's Cave was then in a sorry state of dilapidation with wistful reminders of happier, pre-war days. My favourite violin and piano machine had been wrecked.

*Maurice Packham*

If you go back in the history of Brighton when it was Brighthelmston you had the Eastdeaners and the Westdeaners. Now they call them denes, which are valleys, and therefore the Eastdeaners were more to do with the east side of the Palace Pier, because that's where the dene comes down through there. And if you're a Westdeaner, they were mostly on the Russell Street beaches, because that is the bottom of West Street where another dene comes through there.

And there was always a sort of a family feud if you go back long enough, between the Eastdeaners and the Westdeaners, and the conflict between them you're really going back to the sixteenth and seventeenth centuries. When I first went to market, which is back in the 1930s - there were still some families that wouldn't speak to other families even in those days.

*John Leach* Catching Stories

The Ovetts, they were a fishing family who lived in Frederick Gardens and Frederick Street, are reputed to have come over with what is known as the hog-boats. Now my uncle Bill, who was a Marchant, and his children even up till recently were known as 'Oggies', and I used to think to myself, what a horrible name to have. But it worked out the fact that they were hog-boat fishermen. With the Prince Regent here, they had to find a boat that would land on these Brighton beaches because the French aristocracy wanted to come to Brighton, because of the Prince Regent and the Pavilion. They found the most suitable boats were the pig-boats, which were in the canals of France for the transport of pigs. And when they came over they came ashore in the surf so well on the Brighton beach, the Brighton fishermen adopted them. And the fishermen in them were known as Oggies.

*Joe Mitchell* Catching Stories

*A family enjoying their beach hut on Hove seafront in 1931*

*Advertising teas in the 1930s*

The days would always end for us in the same way. As the crowds left in the evening, we would start a beach comb. Searching for comics left over by indulged children - it was absolute ecstasy if we found an American comic - empty lemonade bottles, to claim the penny deposit back at the seafront shops, also if we were very lucky we would pick up a tea tray complete with cutlery and china. The deposit on these ranged from between 1/6d and 2/6d so we did very well. Our bubble burst when the cafe lady recognised us and decided to save herself 2/6d. She really should have waited until the tray was on the counter. Being an awkward little bugger, I dropped the lot on the floor and ran.

*Dave Huggins*

The lawns on the seafront from First Avenue to Fourth Avenue were owned by the West Brighton Estate and were fenced in. Flower beds were planted according to the season. Under the ground was a pump which pumped sea water to all the houses on the estate. The grass was cut by a mowing machine pulled by one of W Miles' horses, who, to stop the lawn being damaged, wore leather boots fitted over his hooves. My part was to collect the cuttings for disposal. These lawns, being private, could only be used by the residents on the estate who had keys. After the war the Council took them over and of course they are now part of the Brunswick Lawns.

*Ernie Mason* A Working Man

In the summer some of the kids, girls as well, used to go barefooted on nice days, so their parents could save on the shoe leather. To be in fashion, I left my boots and shoes off, and used to go with my pals down to the Banjo Groyne beach - the tide seemed to go out further then - and go bathing with clothes or swimming costumes on, girls as well, but they kept well away from us.

On the way back some of the very poor children used to look for what they called Chockers; that was an apple core not eaten very much, or perhaps an orange that had only been partly sucked. The lucky finder would have first bite, and then hand it over to the next one, and so on, until it was all gone, pips and all.

*Bert Healey*

*Pascal Biscuits works outing on the Palace Pier in 1930*

When we lived in Carlton Street as schoolboys, when dad was herring-catching, we used to have to get up four or five o'clock in the morning, school time, go down the beach and get half a prickel of herrings, which would be about a hundred big herrings. We'd come home and we'd put them in a tub of brine - a waterproof tub - soak them, and go to school where you'd got herring scales on your hands, not washed properly and you get a donk off the headmaster for that, coming dirty. And then you go home dinnertimes and you'd get these herrings and stick them on a stick, you might put thirty on a stick, and then you'd put them in herring dees - we used to use a dog kennel, cleaned out when the herring season come, scrub it clean, and we used to use that - and smoke these herrings and make bloaters of them. And we used to have to do that when we come home at teatime from school.

*Johnny Humphrey* Catching Stories

She was a fine, lovely girl, well-made, lovely teeth, and fair, bobbed hair. We used to go to the pictures. She had one full day off a month, half a day off every week, and on Sundays, what was called an early night off. I used to meet her mostly on her half day or Sunday evenings. I could not manage a full day off.

She used to like a port and lemon, and we would perhaps go on to the West or Palace Pier if it was a fine night, have a dance, watch the Pierrot show, and go into the bar. I would have a pint of shandy and she her port and lemon and if we had another one, she always insisted on paying.

*Bert Healey*

It was around the Spring of 1932 when I started courting Dorothy. I used to serve her Mother and called every day. I had seen Dorothy several times when calling at her house and I had an idea that she used to go along the seafront. There was a lovely beach at Paston Place for bathing where I did bump into her but she had her bike with her. So after chatting for a while, we started walking towards the Pier and as I lived in Coombe Road we walked the rest of the way to her home and I was the one pushing the bike.

The following day I asked her Mother if I could walk out with her daughter. She said she had no objections and that was how it all started. Dorothy used to work at J Lyons and I used to meet her on her way to work. Every day, she used to have two lovely cream doughnuts for her lunch which she never paid for. We got married on Boxing Day in 1936 after a very good courtship.

*George Grout* The Smiling Bakers

*Near the Palace Pier, 1930s*

When we were children, especially me, we wanted to earn a little bit of pocket money, so I used to stay at the bottom of Chuters Gardens in West Street and wait for the all day trippers to come down from London. I used to have a little board there saying 'Wash and brush up threepence, toilet a penny'. My mother used to have this great big tin bath right by the toilet with a platform on where they could have a wash and brush up. That would cost them threepence.

We used to go winkling at Black Rock and we got the winkles all crawling, bring them home and my mother put them into a great big tub on the gas and they were all climbing up the sides, she'd cook them and we would eat them. My mother was a champion winkle picker and she used to get a hair pin out of her hair and get them out. You would find her with all these little black spots all over her with the heads of the winkles.

*Margaret Newman* Catching Stories

There was a high-class restaurant called Chatfields just round the corner in West Street. In those days, in the front window would be a little waterfall, a kind of little stream with live eels swimming in it. Customers could pick which eel they fancied and have it cooked whichever way they liked by the chef. Sometimes they would have a small orchestra at weekends, with violinist, accordion, drums and Wally on the piano. The musicians might change, but it was always Wally who played the piano. He must have been good, because Chatfields then was very high-class. Sometimes Happy would give Wally a break on the piano. He played by ear. He could knock a fair tune out and to be different he would sometimes play by his fists, using his knuckles.

*Bert Healey*

Outside [my parents'] pub we had several advertising boards, which entitled us to two free seats once a fortnight. My friend and I were given these tickets. We could go to matinees on the piers (there was a theatre on both the Palace Pier and the West Pier) or the first house of the Hippodrome. After going to the latter we used to buy fish and chips at Silverthornes at 6d, but if we weren't in by 9.00pm then we were in trouble.

The two piers were a great source of entertainment and in 1928, when my friend and I were both twenty, we used to spend a lot of time on them. I preferred the West Pier: it wasn't as long as the Palace Pier, but I liked the more sedate atmosphere. It was kept in beautiful condition and after the ravages of the sea and the weather of winter, there began a grand spring cleaning effort, where underparts were checked for damage before the arrival of the paddle steamers each Easter. The paintwork was then restored and any worn planking replaced.

*Marjory Batchelor* A Life Behind Bars

David Sewell

**I LOVED GOING ON THE TWO PIERS**. Brighton Palace Pier was my favourite; the West Pier was more for the adults to enjoy. In those days you had to pay to go onto the piers. The Palace Pier had more machines to play on, at a penny a go. I don't remember ever winning any money on these machines. Some of the machines had flicking, moving pictures which was very exciting especially one called 'What the Butler Saw'. I did not really understand the story it was telling, but found the adults were laughing, especially the ladies who giggled when viewing this machine. As to the present-day machines, I am sure my granny would have been horrified, "Evil devils!" she would have exclaimed.

There was a very different atmosphere then, people appeared to get lots of pleasure from experiencing simple things: just walking the length of the pier, down one side and back up the other; sitting watching the sea and people on the beaches below. I always wore my Sunday best when we went on the piers.

Every summer they held a Bathing Belles Carnival competition on the Palace Pier. The pier was usually crowded on the day it was held. Mother had a friend, Dorothy, who used to enter the competition. One year she came third and the adults had tea in the posh cafe near the end of the pier and I was given a large ice cream in a dish.

*Barbara Chapman* Boxing Day Baby

Every year in August, Dad bought Mum a new summer hat ready for the Bank Holiday outing. So wet Bank Holidays were black days, as Mum came home bad tempered with a ruined floppy hat, and we were all as miserable as the weather. But often the sun shone, so we walked to the seafront, and watched the antics of the London daytrippers disgorging from their coaches, or char-a-bancs, as they were called. Then we went on the Palace Pier, but were not allowed to waste money on the slot machines, so we never knew what the butler saw, and besides the view-finder was placed too high to peer into.

However, some of the animated theatre scenes such as "The Haunted House" were free for all to see. There was a palmist and a stunt-man, who dived through flames into the sea. There was a tearoom and an orchestra, a family show in the theatre, and ballroom dancing behind screens at the end of the Palace Pier, near the jetty where the paddlesteamers came in. On rare occasions Dad took us all on the steamer to Eastbourne or the Isle of Wight, and I still remember the excitement of clattering down the iron steps of the landing stage, with the siren sounding.

*Ruby Dunn* Moulsecoomb Days

Another treat was going with Granny on the paddle steamers which we boarded on the end of the Palace Pier. I was fascinated by the engine room, where I could see the large paddles going round when the boat began to move and all the highly-polished brass machinery. The best trip was going to the Isle of Wight.

My mother used to take us on the coach trips, which commenced near the Palace Pier. These were mostly taken in the afternoons when the coaches displayed a blackboard stating where they were going. I loved the mystery trips, these usually went into the countryside, where we ended the tour in a tea garden.

Along the seafront near the bandstand just past the West Pier, there used to be donkey rides and a Punch and Judy Show. I would stay and watch for a long time if my mother allowed me. I never became tired of watching and laughing at this remarkable show. I still watch Punch and Judy if I ever see one being performed.

*Barbara Chapman*

A lot of the girls joined the Brighton Ladies Swimming Club, and we produced a good team and won the Schools Shield. We used to enter for the Regattas off the West Pier, and the Pier to Pier races. One year six of us entered for this event. It took place on a Saturday afternoon. We did very well. One of the girls came first and a couple of us got prizes, which was a good result, as there were quite a lot of entrants.

My brother Bill also took part in the West Pier Galas and the men's "Pier to Pier", and also races round the Pier. His friend was Jimmy Godwin of Hove Shiverers Club and many times I have seen them race against each other and come in to finish with their arms round each others necks.

*Olive Masterson* The Circle of Life

*Margaret Boniface*

*Bathers at Hove in 1931*

Go down the Fishmarket, and a lot of the poor kids would go 'Happy Jacking'. They'd go down the Fishmarket, and they'd sing to the people walking along the seafront, and people would throw them pennies. I suppose they didn't have much food, and they were poor, really poor.

*Doris Watherington* Catching Stories

As kids we used to sing under the pier, at the visitors strolling on the pier, hoping they would throw us coins. How we managed to find the coins among the stones I do not know. We used to get strict instructions from mum not to do it, and if we were found out we were reprimanded, or got a good clout.

*Mavis Cameron* Back Street Brighton

When Stephen was our only child at school, and fast growing into a young man, taller than his father and at an awkward age, they used to go fishing. Jack really enjoyed that. He wanted to be a friend to his son as well as a father. They would go to the Palace Pier, until one day Stephen caught his line on a dead body. A lady had committed suicide. Poor Stephen was very shaken, and it was a number of years before he went there again.

*Olive Masterson*

And once a year they'd have the carnival. That would be in the summer. Down by the Pier all the boats would go out and they'd dress them with all their fairy lights.

*Doris Watherington*

It used to start off with me and the old man, he'd be in bed in the afternoon and he'd get up and the old lady would say, 'Where you going Jim?' 'I'm going to shove off,' he says. That would be when they used to go late autumn fishing when the herring were just coming in. And the little boats on the beach, the fourteen-footers, they'd go out, just at dusk you know, and get out to where the fishing grounds were. He'd go out in the evening and come back about three o'clock in the morning, after shoaling.

*James Ward* Catching Stories

I might have been about four or five. In them days while you were still at school - well, you more or less had to go with your father. And when we left school it was automatic, you went fishing, and then when you was capable you used to take charge of the boat. I went full-time fishing, for about four years, and that was for the whole season: the herring season, the mackerel season, trammel season, and trawling.

*Johnny Humphrey*

Joe Leach was known as 'Smokey Joe'. Face was always black. These old fishermen, people used to say how dirty they was, but when you come to think about it, these boats, they had their little old fire in the cabin, and they had a boiler, and you've got these two chimneys coming up out on deck just in front of the skipper who's steering the vessel, and there's all this smoke, all about face height, they used to get black.

And the poor blighters, when they was drifting they never had water enough to wash, because they only used to take a keg of water to sea with them, and they was always drinking tea, they never had water for washing.

*Bob Holden* Catching Stories

Wherever you went through the town, you would come across a variety of banjo strummers, violinists, mouth organ blowers or barrel-organ grinders. Wild rumours went around about the amount of money they collected, it was even whispered that some of 'em were millionaires. Comparing their takings with the average working man's wages at the time, perhaps some of them did very well. But by the look of them, I don't imagine that many looked far beyond tomorrow's beer money.

A notable exception was the two Italian gents who toured the streets with a full sized harp, a stool, and a violin. These men were real musicians, and covered a wide area of Brighton and Hove. During the summer-season they played the pleasure-steamers that took trips from the Palace Pier. It is easy to believe that these two made lots of money. They made beautiful music, and were worth every penny.

*Sid Manville* Everything Seems Smaller

You had the breakwater, you had the East Pier light and the West Pier light. And the West Pier light always used to change colours because of the depth of the water. And when a steamer was coming in they'd change it over for a white light for to coast her up the harbour, but if there was something coming down the harbour they'd have a red light up on the watch house, so they'd stop any coming in so the other one would have room to go out.

You know where the lift is on the front, there was two red lights on that, that was the main marker. And then down the bottom of Bedford Street, on the left-hand side, there's a triangle, of lights, that was Old Ben's Lights. That was my grandfather, old Ben Allen. It was right where all the boats used to come ashore and heave up, that was the mark for them.

*'Big Ted' Gillam* Catching Stories

All our relatives were at sea. I had a great-uncle that was lost at sea, on a very calm night, as the ship was coming about the boom caught him and knocked him overboard. In those days the fishermen wore very heavy leather boots to keep them on deck in any rough weather. Not like the rubber ones of today. And therefore he never stood a chance of swimming.

*Jim Sinden* Catching Stories

At the end of the West Pier was a theatre, which put on a variety of good plays six evenings a week, and two matinees. In the middle of the pier was the Winter Garden, rather like a huge conservatory, with plants and potted palms everywhere. Here an orchestra would play afternoons and evenings. One conductor was called Jimmy Sale, a great exhibitionist who appeared in full evening dress with white gloves and who attracted many ladies. Later, open-air dancing was introduced at the end of the pier and, weather permitting, we danced to gramophone records. We'd be protected by a high canvas windbreak with an attendant at the opening to see that no-one got in without paying.

*A family on Brighton beach in the summer of 1938*

That was life on the West Pier until around 1940 when the centre of both piers were blown up to prevent attempted enemy landings.

*Marjory Batchelor*

**THE BEACHES HAD BEEN MINED** and barricaded with barbed wire, which stretched for miles along the coast. Even the two beautiful piers had been blown up in the middle. I never saw the logic of that demolition. In the pre-war days I had loved to wander on the piers, even though you had to pay. I loved it especially at night when they lit up the sky with a myriad of twinkling lights. Now, all that had gone, along with the gaiety and fun. All we were left with was the blackout.

*Kathleen Wilson* International Service

When the Germans occupied France in the summer of 1940 Brighton became a front-line town under direct threat of invasion from the sea. As part of their general invasion of England German planners considered a parachute landing on the South Downs to cover a seaborne attack on Brighton. On the British side plans were made to defend Brighton and evacuate the town if the Germans invaded. Bank staff were informed that, if the Germans landed during office hours, they would not be able to contact their families, but would be evacuated with the bank's money and papers on a special train from Brighton Station.

Individual citizens were told that when the invasion was signalled by the ringing of church bells, they should keep off the roads (to free them for military traffic) and walk towards London wearing bright clothing, so they would not be shot by mistake as advancing German soldiers. The ill-armed Home Guard and army must have waited anxiously behind the barbed wire and mines planted along Brighton sea front, until the summer of 1941, when the Germans marched east against the Russians and the threat of invasion was lifted.

*Michael Corum* Brighton Behind the Front

*Sandbagging the Aquarium and Prince's Hall, 1939*

And underneath the walk, along by the Aquarium, there was big, massive tanks of petrol, ready to roll into the sea, to set the sea alight in case of invasion. I suppose they must have held about ten thousand gallons. They were all the way along underneath the promenade.

*George Heffaran* Brighton Behind the Front

Us local kids bitterly resented the summer influx of thousands of day trippers. London by the sea they called our beloved town. The trippers used to swarm into Queens Road from the trains, so many at times that they nearly stopped the trams. On they swept past the Clock Tower down West Street and onto the seafront.

Like lemmings, the majority would turn left - easily explainable, before them the panorama of countless pubs cafes and ice cream parlours. Along the lower promenade, all the joys of holiday makers with their accompanying delicious odours. Stalls and shops selling Brighton Rock in all shapes and sizes, toothache by the yard. Candy floss, jellied eels, cockles and whelks, fish and chips smothered in onion vinegar, what ambrosia. Silly hats with "KISS ME QUICK" and many very saucy postcards. The jingling sound of little donkeys plodding along, sometimes carrying too heavy a load. The cries of the boatmen, "Anymore for the Skylark, half way to China for a bob".

Then dead ahead the Palace Pier, with Aladdin's Caves stretching along beneath the upper promenade. The Ghost Train, Hall of Mirrors and slot machines by the thousands. The trippers needed to go no further. The beaches round the Palace Pier and along back to West Street were crowded with them.

Leslie Whitcomb

*Bumper cars on Madeira Drive in 1947*

We locals used to turn right at the bottom of West Street. A parade of small shops and the Palladium Cinema, then the swish hotels, the Grand, Metropole, and others. Over to the other side and even the lower promenade was more refined, less shops and most of the small arches under the pavement were used as beach huts.

The beaches here were cleaner and less crowded, and above all, there was my 'Goddess'; elegant and beautiful, gleaming in her pristine white paint, with eastern type gold minarets on her brow and the white foam of waves breaking at her feet - The West Pier - and I fell in love.

Thinking back, I realise it was not only the architecture that attracted me, it was also possible to get to the first slot machine arcade without paying. When in funds we would spend hours on the pier for a low admission charge. Haunting the slot machines for the chance of a free go, annoying the serious fishermen at the southern end, and watching the rich go aboard the paddle steamer for a trip in the Channel. Never got bored, then in my thirteenth year, war was declared.

Did not seem to make a lot of difference until suddenly the British Expeditionary Force was in full retreat and falling back on the French town of Dunkirk. Everything on Brighton beach that could float left to assist in one of the greatest seaborne rescues of an army that will ever be recorded. But worst of all for me, they blew a bloody great hole in my darling.

The powers that be said it was required to prevent the German Army using it as a landing stage if they invaded. Imagine a hole in the Pier holding up the seemingly invincible Wehrmacht for long. What nonsense, all they needed was to leave the normal bloke in the booth. If the Germans had not got the right money, they would never have got past him. We tried for years and failed.

*Dave Huggins*

Eddie, that's my husband, told me once when they put their nets down they thought they had got a good catch, so they hauled the net in and it was a German pilot, still sitting in the cockpit of his plane, fully dressed in his flying uniform - not a pretty sight. They said, 'Let him go, nets and all.' Anyway, it tore their nets to bits, which wasn't very good.

*Dorothy Pierce* Catching Stories

We was fishing just off of Black Rock here, and we caught a machine gun, and I took it down to our old arch and I cleaned it all up and well, I should think you could have got it working. And the police came down there one day and they took it away from me, and one of them come over and told me, he said, 'It's a marvellous thing, it was a German one, and if he was firing on an English ... he was lucky,' because one of the shells had been jammed in, he might have got blown up, you know, shot down, because his machine gun never worked.

*'Big Ted' Gillam*

They took her to sea out of Shoreham, as they went out of the harbour they went off in a gale, and the sea turned them over, they'd only two crew, which was another relative, Marchant, and Mitchell. The family story is - and I believe it to be true because I've heard it so many times in my life - Marchant came ashore in Shoreham, they picked his body up, put him on a barrow, wheeled him back to Brighton up to Nelson Street where my great-grandfather lived, threw stones at the window 'cos it was night-time, and called up, 'Widow Marchant! Widow Marchant!' and she put her head out the window and said, 'I'm not a widow!' and they said, 'Well, you are now, your old man's body's here on the barrow!' My father identified the other body which was found two weeks later. It had come up the hole under the groyne of the Palace Pier and was found at the bottom of St. James' Street in the sewer there - it was two weeks old, that's what I can remember, little instances that stay in your mind.

*Joe Mitchell*

There was a lot of swimming I remember from my childhood. The fun swimming was at Black Rock (now Brighton Marina), where there was an outdoor swimming pool with boards and outdoor table-tennis and you could go down to a `private beach' and there were rock-pools and ice-creams. It was like being in Butlin's for a day. Anyhow, I had been a habitué of the seafront since my first winter of 1946-47 when we lived by Morgan's the chemists in Arundel Road. Here

Esther Georgiles

*Near Hove bandstand in 1944*

Leslie Whitcomb

*The Madeira lift on Brighton seafront in 1950*

my mum got round the electricity cuts by boiling-up water on the gas-ring, putting hot-water bottles in my pram and running up and down the seafront. That way she kept herself warm as well. I got the feeling that Black Rock served mainly that end of town. People did not leap into cars and travel miles from Hove for their pleasures. They did not have cars and outings like Black Rock were memorable because they were exceptional.

*Andy Steer* Brighton Boy

We did have little trips. There was an aircraft carrier, the Indefatigable, that was moored off the end of the Palace Pier and we had trips to go out to that. That must have been about '48/49.

*Roy Page* School Reports

One of our boats caught a sturgeon. It has to be offered to the Queen if a sturgeon's caught. She refused it so we had it ourselves. I suppose it was about the late forties. If they catch an unusual fish they like to keep it alive in a bucket of salt water, because they would sell them to the Aquarium and put them in the tanks there. When they catch unusual fish - that's how they were disposed of.

*Johnny Leach*

If a blue nosed shark, or a pug nosed shark, was caught in the nets they used to take it out, keep that net but find an old net, wrap the shark in, put it on a barrow and tell the public that the shark has bitten all the nets and torn them to pieces purposely to get more money.

*Rene Taylor* Catching Stories

Margaret Boniface

Maureen Middlemiss

*Brighton seafront in the 1950s*

**THERE WAS THE LOVELY CONCERT HALL** [on the West Pier] which catered for five hundred people when it was full, which it often was in the height of the season. It was waitress service. There was the Ocean Restaurant for six hundred. It was really nice and it used to be filled with people every morning in the bay looking out to sea. Like being on board ship. There was also the West Bar and the East Bar, both licensed, and amusements.

The Pier was seldom short of staff as they came back year after year for their jobs. It was one big happy family. I realised after working a season that the cleanliness and appearance of the Pier was due to the hard work done in the off-season period by the pier master and deckhands. Also during winter they checked and repaired the decking. There was also a team of divers who came every year to repair damaged girders and pylons, so we all felt very safe. It was a credit to all concerned. Every season it was as though it had had a spring clean. The sea end had quite a lot of little shops: candy floss, popcorn, fortune tellers, shellfish, cockles and mussels - various shops. The people who rented the small shops came back every year to sell their wares and enjoy the happy atmosphere.

I thought it would be quite frightening working over the sea, strange thing was you never noticed it. Several times I saw porpoises basking in the sea. The first time I thought they were whales.

*Daphne Mitchell* Oh What a Lovely Pier

37

In the fifties, one of the big things about Brighton was the Arts Ball and it was held at the Aquarium. And it was really quite something. It was known all over England. In fact we used to say that a certain number of queans used to spend the whole of the summer sitting on the Men's Beach, sewing sequins on the gowns. And they sewed them on by the hundredweight, not by the dozen.

The Aquarium was quite a big place and it held about a hundred, I suppose. At first they turned a blind eye to anybody in drag but then it got a little bit hilarious and they wouldn't permit drag for the last two or three years and finally it was shut. But it was really quite hilarious, it was from about nine or ten at night to about two or three in the morning. It was extremely well-run. There was no trouble. They didn't have any bash-ups or people throwing chairs.

Some of the costumes must have cost hundreds. It was fantastic. I mean, ostrich feathers in those days when the salaries were £5 a week, some of those ostrich feathers were seven pounds, just one feather, and they probably had twenty on a headgear. Quite a big thing, the Arts Ball.

*Grant at the Arts Ball*

*Grant* Daring Hearts

When I was a child Black Rock boasted a magnificent pool with deckchairs all round the edge, and a paddling pool at one end of the enclosure. We spent many happy hours playing in the water, sometimes just we two, sometimes with friends and the best bit was that Mum and Dad would often join in. They both enjoyed swimming and tried to teach us the art of diving as well, to no avail I'm afraid: neither Bert nor I ever got to grips with diving, an inelegant belly flop was the best we achieved, but Black Rock Pool was a Mecca to us. Sadly, it no longer exists, it was destroyed in the name of progress to make way for Brighton Marina.

*Janis Ravenett* Snapshots

On the east side of Banjo Groyne, you used to have to go down steps to get to the beach. Under the Volk's Railway there was steps went down, and the water used to come right up there. People used to sit there and have something to eat if it was calm. That was always called the Lido because they used to have floodlight bathing there. and I bet if anybody dug down on them piles what the railway runs on, they'd find the old floodlights, what they used to have for floodlight bathing.

*Johnny Humphrey*

We had summers then, didn't we? Nearly every day we went boating, to make ends meet. Brighton was loaded with people. One go in a row boat: six pence. But you charged two bob if you were aboard a Tradeboat. You was only s'posed to carry twelve but this Board of Trade boat I had, she carried twenty-eight. If you got a pound a day, you was lucky. Then you'd go up the beer shop and spend it!

*'Cow Heel' Andrew* Catching Stories

They came from all over the country, London, all over, you name it - a day's outing to Brighton. And they used to come down, and wander around the town, and come down the beach, and have two or three drinks up the pubs, and do a knees-up on the beach, they'd dance all round the beach, and they'd have a trip out in the boat. They was always in a good mood, you could always talk them into a ride in the boat. Used to have some saucy sailors, mind, 'If you're going to be sick, make sure you fall out the boat and get sick over the side.'

Course, the kids, they always wanted to go in the boat. Used to get mothers and fathers to come down to us and say, 'Here's our three kids, let them stop with you a couple hours,' and pay you so they can go up and have a drink, and be on their own, like. We used to have people come down when it was Brighton racing, with their kids, if it was a fine day, and they pushed their kids down to us, 'Let them stop with you all day, we're going up Brighton races.'

*Ted Watherington* Catching Stories

We took the number forty-two bus from the Pepperbox to St James Street and then walked down Rock Gardens to the sea front. Once safely over the busy main road, we four children ran ahead of the grown-ups. Helter-skelter we hurled ourselves along to the top of the huge flight of steps and here we stopped and took a deep breath. Then, eyes alight with the joy of it all, we caught our first glimpse of the sparkling water. Nothing ever compared to that first glimpse, and I still get the same thrill today every time I stand at that spot and look at the sea with the Palace Pier striding proudly out onto the ocean.

Stopping only to purchase shiny new buckets and spades we hurried along looking for just the right spot to settle. It must be near the water's edge - not too near if the tide was coming in, and it must be fairly flat so that the mums could sit in comfort. They never wasted money on deck chairs. After much discussion we all agreed that we had found the perfect spot and we four children literally tore our clothes off and plunged into the water.

*Janis Ravenett*

When I just started work on the West Pier, I was part-time. Then, after a while, my day started at 10am till 10pm, six days a week. Also I usually worked my day off, plus some of my holidays. We were open Christmas Day and Boxing Day, right through to the next season. That was quite an experience. When it snowed, it was like working on a desert island: toilets frozen up and no water until we thawed some for tea. It was hilarious, we had to save the water and have one wash-up every now and again. There was a tank and when I needed water I just used to go and get a lump of ice.

One day I was rolling a ten-gallon churn of milk; there is a way of rolling them. The lid came off and the ten gallons poured out all over the Concert Hall floor. I was petrified. The supervisor came in. She said, 'What are you worried about? It's lucky to spill milk.' I got off lightly!

*Daphne Mitchell*

*Children by the Palace Pier in 1952*

Oh, the freedom, the fresh air, the space, the wonderful, wonderful water. Swimming, paddling, resting, eating sandwiches, the time passed in a happy blur till, best of all, that breathtaking moment when you put your feet down in the water - almost but not quite out of your depth - and felt with your toes - SAND!

"Ruth, Ruth, the sand's coming in." The cry died on my lips, some moments are just too precious to share, and this I must keep to myself for just a few moments until the others found out for themselves - this was my most magical secret. I turned away to hide my smiles and hugged my ecstasy to myself. I never could understand that it was the water that moved and not the sand, but I can still vividly remember that feeling of joy and of not wanting to share it with anyone else.

*Drinking Pepsi on the beach in August 1960*

Herb Goulden

At last as the sun set in the soft blue sky we gathered up all our bits and pieces, all the seaweed and precious pebbles we had gathered during our day on the beach and set off to make our way home. The long walk up the pebbles, the climbing of the huge flight of steps, trailing up Rock Gardens to the bus stop, buckets and spades clutched in our tired hands - completely worn out but totally, totally happy.

*Janis Ravenett*

Ken Lyon played for the music hall. I think he played on the [West] Pier for about eight seasons - a very nice man. I used to love the afternoon sessions when he would sometimes ask us if we had any requests for him to play. The music certainly helped to keep everyone going when it became a madhouse, and often chaotic. Sometimes they would run out of teapots, they couldn't get them washed quick enough. We didn't use tea bags then, so it was a case of all hands on deck and do anything to ease the situation.

*Daphne Mitchell*

Brighton was the humming place. First and foremost, there was the Men's Beach. There was so much beauty down there, I mean, you had to have binoculars to get it all in. It was too fantastic. Everybody knew about the Men's Beach. There was nothing in the rest of the country to compare. So of course, all these people that came down on holiday, they just went down, if the weather was fine, they probably slept there all night.

If you went far enough down, there was no such thing as wearing any clothing, and it was quite a wide stretch of beach too. And on a weekend in the summer, you literally had to find a spot about a foot square. And you just walked around and when you found somebody that hadn't got a friend, or wasn't talking, you sat yourself down, and started chatting away. And if you didn't click. well, you got up and you walked around again.

*The opening of the official Brighton Naturist Beach on 1 April 1980*

So it was a continuous circle of people walking around, and suddenly sitting, then upping and round again. It was quite amusing. It was men only. If there were any women or children strayed on it they were promptly told to get off. Lots of very famous and infamous people could have been photographed on the Men's Beach, I can assure you.

The reason that it was shut after many, many years, I'm talking about probably twenty or thirty years, was because along there the police convalescent home had some police huts and the police came along one day and bulldozed the sign down. That was the end of the Men's Beach. They have never ever got anything quite like it in Brighton since. I mean the nudist beach, right up at the Marina, is nothing compared to that old Men's Beach.

*Grant*

I remember I had a party [on the West Pier] for two hundred and fifty old-age pensioners. The afternoons were hectic enough without parties, of which I had about fifty at odd days during the summer. Sometimes there would be a party for two hundred and fifty fish and chips, bread and butter, cakes and jam, and tea. I went to work extra early on those days to prepare, otherwise it would have been chaos.

I had to count the two hundred and fifty plates, put them on the hot plate, which was temperamental and worked sometimes. All the other jobs connected to the parties had to be done, such as putting on the tea-urns. The way to make the tea was to put two urns on the gas when boiling. Tie some tea in a cloth, secure to the end of a broom handle. Stand on a chair and lift up and down till right colour. It was quite a job as the bundle of tea got heavier. We were told it was a smashing cup of tea!

*Daphne Mitchell*

To my mind the Fishmarket was one of the centres of Brighton. It was the centrepin of the seafront. It was done for political reasons to get it away. They used all these new health regulations as a lever to get the fishermen off Brighton beach and they're still trying to.

*Dave May* Catching Stories

The hotels made a complaint. The smell, the smell of the 'ard but that 'ard was scrubbed down every day but they kept on and on and they moved them out 1960 or 1962 when they went into Circus Street.

*'Cow Heel' Andrew*

Between coming out of the forces at twenty and say, twenty-two, there was a sort of in between period, where I wouldn't accept the fact that I was gay. I was very young and very apprehensive about actually going into a gay bar. We thought how daring this would be. So one night, in the summer, we decided we would go into this gay bar, the Greyhound, opposite the cinema along East Street. We got to the Palace Pier and we walked on and we hadn't got the courage to go in. We got practically to Rottingdean, we still hadn't got the courage.

But on the way back, we said, 'We are going in!' So we came back along the seafront, back to Pool Valley, we came up through that side street and we pushed open the door quickly and Steve and I fell in the door and to our horror, we found we were in the heterosexual bar and the gay bar was upstairs. So I lowered my voice and went, 'Brown ale, please.' Suddenly out of the corner of our eye, we saw all these people trooping upstairs and I can't tell you how much courage it took to walk from that bar, to go up those stairs because what you were actually doing, in front of all those people was saying, 'I'm one of them.'

*George* Daring Hearts

*Looking north from the West Pier entrance on 15 May 1973*

Royal Pavilion and Museums, Brighton & Hove

When I first came to this country I was overjoyed to know that I was going to stay in a seaside town that reminded me of my own town of Naples. After I had been introduced to the family I would be living with, I wanted to see the town. I aimed for the seafront. Although it was August, the promenade and beach seemed deserted. It made me feel nostalgic for my own town. The only comparison I could make was the smell of the sea. In my home town of Naples there would have been lots of people on the beach and swimming in the blue sea under a bright sky. Here, to me, the sea seemed grey and sad. After a while spent in England I got used to the weather and changed my mind about Brighton. Today Brighton is just like home.

*Delia Dumighan* I Do Like to be Beside the seaside

The second time I went into Pigott's, Jess came in and that was the next thirteen years of my life taken care of. She came in and said, 'Hello, would you like a drink?' so I said, 'Yes, please.' So she bought me a drink and asked me what I was doing and who I was with and, 'Have you got anyone?' I said, No.' I don't know at what point she said, 'Well, you're mine now.' She took me down onto the seafront and I was absolutely terrified of being with her 'cause I thought she was going to grab me and take me onto the pebbles and rape me and do all sorts. I was really quite frightened. I think she did eventually kiss me somewhere along the seafront. I was desperately lonely and I wanted someone and I grabbed at the first straw. I'd been on my own for what seemed like so many years that the first person that showed a scrap of warmth towards me, I was theirs.

*Gill* Daring Hearts

Pigeons nest on those girders, under the pier. And when they used to nest there, some of the little ones, the fledglings used to fall out of the nest, and fall in the water, and they couldn't properly fly and my old man used to scramble down the piles and he used to pick them up and put them in a box, and I used to take them home. We sold them to a bloke named West who had a fish shop in Church Street, who kept them for a hobby.

*James Ward*

Ned Hoskins

*The underside of the West Pier in 1982*

I do not know why the board of directors decided to sell it [the West Pier]. There was a lot of speculation but we really did not know. It was very sudden. It must have been drastic as the manager was devastated. He died soon after.

*Daphne Mitchell*

There were some camp people about, I know two or three used to terrify me to death. They used to camp themselves gutless on the seafront at night. I used to have to run up a side street to get out of their way because they knew I was one of the boys. They just flaunted it completely, very, very camp. They were disliked for it, people said, 'Oh, keep away from those awful people.' But there was nothing awful about them, they were just outrageously camp, they'd scream across the road, 'Hello, darling.' Well, in those days you just didn't do that sort of thing.

*Peter* Daring Hearts

We continued with that [pleasure boating] up to '66 and with the decline of that, we had the Edward and Mary, and I bought another boat called the Gannet and we used to do a bit of trammelling and a bit of netting, but mainly we started to take out fishing parties from Shoreham. And then, it would have been 1968 we came to Brighton Marina. I think we were about the first boats to come in here and we went back to doing mainly angling and fishing, but the tripping boats, there's no boats working from the beach at all now. It's all finished.

*Dave May*

My sex life started when I came to Brighton, when I was forty-six. I got a bed-sitter in Temple Street for 25 bob a week and a job on the West Pier selling ice-cream. I used to have a couple of purple hearts, with purple hearts you became less inhibited, and two pints of bitter and walk along the front and the first boy I liked the look of, I used to say, 'Would you like to come home with me?' And more often than not, they said, 'Yes.' They'd always want a pair of socks or shirt or breakfast the next morning and things like that. And they used to get ten bob.

*Eric* Daring Hearts

On my second day in Brighton I got myself this job on the West Pier – Deck-hand. Well, fair enough I suppose, piers have decks as well as ships, although they only have one, usually, plus a few bits and pieces. So I started in next morning at 8am.

There were only two 'deckles', a regular old hand who was in charge, and myself. The regular, Barney, sported a sailor hat and wore something vaguely resembling a uniform and did a variety of jobs, anything and everything, on the spot maintenance of the well-worn structure from one end to the other.

To be fair he was kept pretty busy poking and prodding and bashing the old Victorian pier with a variety of heavy tools. Barney was often to be found, spanner in hand, clinging perilously onto the structures underneath the deck, climbing sideways like some giant crab. The 'big boss' chased him far more than he did me so all in all I suppose Barney did not have a lot to laugh about.

Yes, we did have a 'proper' boss, the Pier Manager, this white-collar bloke about fifty all gut and pomp who came over two or three times a day from the hotel opposite; the management there owned the pier. This guy just came and went and didn't stay around enough to bother us (me anyway) too much which was just as well because on occasions, like all bosses, he could be a pig.

*Arthur Thickett* Deckhand, West Pier

**BRIGHTON'S PIERS PLAYED A BIG ROLE** in my childhood, growing up in the city - or the co-joined towns of Brighton and Hove, as they were then. I spent many happy days fishing on the grid at the end of the Palace Pier. I would travel by bus, with a rod, a spade, a bucket and a pocket full of coins given to me by my dad for bait. But instead of buying it, I would dig up lugworms in the mudflats at low-tide, then spend the coins on the slot machines. My favourite one was the execution of Mary Antoinette. I endlessly watched the guillotine blade, and her head rolling into the basket beneath. It's a fate I've liked to imagine happening to anyone who irks me, ever since!

I always preferred the Palace Pier, but there was one attraction on the West Pier that intrigued me - an escapologist, The Great Omani. He would pour a gallon of petrol into the sea below, drop a lighted torch into it, then tie himself up in a straightjacket, jump into the flames and - hey presto - untie himself! I would stand and watch him fascinated, wondering what the big deal was about a man who tied himself up, escaping from his own knots! And every time he would yell at me, 'Hey kid, you want to watch me? The minimum price is a tanner!'

I used to spend all day catching small bream and even smaller pout whiting, and proudly carry my catch home on the No. 52 bus, whereupon my mother, to my endless disappointment, would feed the fish to our cat.

*Peter James*

Once it was my privilege to meet an elderly gentleman in his late seventies, by the name of Bert Croyle. In his early days he had worked in London as head electrician in many of the big variety theatres. He knew and had worked with the legendary Great Houdini.

One day, Bert and I were sitting down sipping a glass of wine when he suddenly said, 'You know, I actually saw Houdini perform his famous death jump from West Pier. This was a publicity stunt to advertise his show at the Brighton Hippodrome. He was handcuffed, chained and padlocked and jumped from the pier into the sea and escaped under-water in about two minutes. The pier was packed. What a showman he was that night. As always with Houdini, the theatre was sold out.' I asked Bert how long ago it was that Houdini performed on the West Pier. 'About fifty years ago,' he replied. 'Right,' I said, 'you've just given me an idea for my next stunt. I will perform Houdini's jump from where he performed it on the West Pier, with handcuffs and chains, as he performed it fifty years ago. I will present it as a salute to the memory of the world's all time greatest escapologist.'

On arrival we were in for a shock. A battery of about a dozen cameramen and reporters were waiting for us. It was obvious they had no intention of going away; they had come for my pictures and intended to get them. They soon pointed out, quite correctly, they had as much right to be on the pier as I had. As this was the middle of summer, the pier was packed with excited holiday-makers. Several years earlier, my lovely wife Eileen and I had performed many times on the pier, when I used to perform underwater escapes four or five times a day. So there was nothing new to me in all this.

The pier master, Roy Royston, had insisted that the lifeguards and beach boat should be present in case something went wrong. He had a diving stage rigged up for me on the pier and on the beach. Changing, I carried my handcuffs and chains and mounted the diving stage to get ready for the jump. There was one big snag: the sea was rough. This did not worry me at all. I had performed in much rougher seas. The trouble was, was it too rough for them to launch the beach life-boat? Time and time again they launched it and time and time again the waves crashed into it, flinging it back onto the beach, often turning it over. If they could launch it and get it away from the beach they would be all right.

Getting it out off the beach was the hard part. It was decided to postpone the stunt for one hour in the hope that the sea would calm down a bit. Eventually there was a lull and the lifeboat was launched with two lifeguards in it.

The whole length of the side of the pier was black with people waiting to see the jump. As I stood on the diving stage, crowds pressed round. Crowds were also gathering on the beach. I wondered to myself whether fifty years ago the scene had been much the same when Houdini had stood here, chained and handcuffed, waiting to jump in the sea. I also wondered if the sea had been as rough on that day.

Soon they had finished chaining and handcuffing me. They had done a very good job. Not many people thought that I could escape out of that lot on land, never mind underwater. I was now standing on the diving stage ready to take the plunge. The lifeboat was hovering off the pier riding the large waves comfortably, the lifeguards looking a little worried. The cameras were all in position ready to catch me as I took the plunge down into the sea, forty feet below, just as Houdini had done fifty years earlier. The Mirror, The Express and many others waited with their cameras.

Finally, to the chorus of '5-4-3-2-1-jump!' I jumped, making a perfect landing into a big wave and disappeared underwater with my friends the fish, who I swim with during the day and eat at night but they don't know this. I remained underwater for about ninety seconds and surfaced again, free of my shackles.

It was nice to look up and see hundreds of happy faces applauding me. It was nice to see the national press taking pictures. It was nice to be able to honour the Great Houdini after fifty years. It was very nice to be able to slide back into the pier bar, for the last time, and to find my old friend Professor Cullen and the press had the drinks lined up for me.

*Ron Cunningham* The Great Omani - The Crowd Roars

Saturday nights I would contrive to get away 'early' – 9.00pm. Most Saturdays I'd have a good old pub crawl – I'd earned it. A quick change and clean-up on the job and I'd sail forth with bells on. After brief calls here and there, perhaps Chatfields and The Ship, I'd finish up at the Belvedere, located right on the sea front under the higher promenade. Frankly, a somewhat sleazy place, it was my usual destination Saturday nights.

*Arthur Thickett*

There was this bar, the Belvedere along Brighton seafront, underneath the arches and sometimes some of the girls used to go in there, and so did sailors and people like that. Well, we went in this bar one night, my girlfriend and I, and I expect one or two others. There were some sailors in there who'd been drinking, and one of them got stroppy and started to have a go at my girlfriend and she must have been quaking in her shoes because he was a great, beefy, muscular character, you know, and he was really quite aggressive. He was standing there and swaying around and threatening her and swinging his fists around and telling her what he was planning to do to her ... And I jumped up, in all my feminine clothes and I stood between him and her and I said, 'Over my dead body you will!' One of his mates came up and said, 'Come on, leave the lesbians alone.' And they walked away, so that was lucky.

*Sandie* Daring Hearts

*Holdiaymakers on the beach at Black Rock*

There was a great character there named Jimmy Allett who used to make net bags for people to take their shopping home in. He used to get a queue of people there and he'd stand there yarning to them and making these net bags. There was two or three of them doing that. All the fishermen used to be there working, just doing their job. For the holiday-makers it was a great entertainment.

*Dave May*

*The fairground either side of the West Pier in 1982*

My first job in a morning was to hose down the shore-end of the pier, the scruffy flotsam and jetsam candy-floss end. I'd complete this task a few minutes before half-eight, when the pier was opened to the early strollers. Next I would put up the big flags, eight in all: the little flags strung in rows stayed up constantly; the big flags came down overnight for preservation; they also came down during daylight hours if the weather became extreme; a rare thing that summer.

After the first few days when, quite frankly, I had the wind-up, it came easy and I thoroughly enjoyed climbing around with the early sun on my shirtless back taking in the view from the high-points as I flew the flags. At dusk I took 'em all down again (the job entailed long hours) showing off a bit if one or two youngish females were around.

*Arthur Thickett*

Mr P. would often give me a few coppers for my trouble and I would use them in the slot machines on the Pier. My favourite game was dislodging the black cats from the wall with ball-bearings from a pistol. This was one of the wonderful old penny-in-the-slot machines which were moved from the West Pier when it closed in the early seventies and set up in The Penny Machine Museum near the end of the Palace Pier, from whence they were moved to one of the King's Road Arches. My own children loved to play on this machine. One cat had the same nick in the ear I remembered as a child.

*Andy Steer*

My job was to help keep the Great British Public happily supplied with booze on a hot-Brighton-August-Bank-Holiday-evening – a daunting prospect…

The Man said. "Just get down there on that tap and fill glasses, jus' keep on fillin' an' fillin'."

"Right," I replied, "just gotta' wash me hands first, though; been emptying rubbish, see. Where's—"

"Don' mind that! Wash 'em in the beer!" He meant it.

That shook me a bit, but what could I do... ? Half-turning I caught the woman's eye. Mary, I knew her by sight. She grinned at me in mid-flight, at the same time nodding frantically at me - 'get-on-with-it.'…

*Arthur Thickett*

We all jumped off the end of the pier I remember once, as a dare, on New Year's Eve. It was horrendous, reported, I believe, in the Evening Argus at the time. My mother was furious yet again, all these dykes picked up on Brighton beach by the coastguard. I lost a shoe, I was most upset about that. I remember I had a false hairpiece, they were quite fashionable at the time, big sort of tall hairdos, and it came off in the sea, with my shoe, which is probably on a Parisian beach by now or wherever the other side of Brighton Channel is. I don't know, mad as hatters. It was freezing too, it was snowing I believe, bloody freezing. We just all did it for a dare, about six or seven of us.

*The Red Arrows flying above the Palace Pier in 1980*

The ambulance came and we were all taken off to some hospital there to see if any of us had suffered a heart attack. Sobered us up, we could have killed ourselves, I mean it was just outrageous. Anyway they released us, they thought we'd probably be alright but we'd got nowhere to go, had we, we hadn't got any money, of course we'd spent it all, and we'd still got a lot of alcohol in us, anyway we were dragged off to the police station and spent the night in cells, where I might say, the WPC's at the time plied us with even more booze, telling us it would warm us up. It was New Year of course. I'm sure they knew we were gay, and I'm sure they were too, definitely, yes. Oh, it was fun, just jumped off the end of the pier, fortunately the tide was up.

*Janice* Daring Hearts

August bank holiday – a thronging West Pier. Out of a brilliant, clear blue sky they came, streaking past in vivid-red silence, followed next instant by a massive roar. The Red Arrows. First in a diamond wedge tight as a fist they looped, then line ahead they looped again, flashing a few dozen feet over our pier before buzzing the Palace Pier.

Two clever-devils broke away and did breathtaking and obviously dangerous feats while the other seven played above, all now using multi-coloured smoke-trails; overall a fantastic spectacle. Soon the most hair-raising stunt of the clever devil duo unfolded. One of the pair flew east beyond the Palace Pier whilst the other went west, away from our overcrowded pleasure-planks. Then, simultaneously, they both executed a tight U-turn and set course, one for our West Pier, the other for the Palace Pier, losing height as they approached.

Each zoomed a score or so feet above their respective piers, still sharply losing height! - thus heading at the water and... pointed directly at each other! Then, almost zero feet above the water they levelled off, still heading directly at each other over that stretch of water between the two piers. At the last possible instant they banked sideways, one right one left, thus flashing their underbellies by each other, wingtips almost skimming the water. I distinctly recall leaning on the pier rail looking DOWN at the two planes executing this manoeuvre, more than once, streaming fabulous multi-coloured smoke. Another trick was for the whole nine, line ahead, to zoom between the two most prominent high-rise buildings - the Metropole and Grand, I think - on the seafront.

*Arthur Thickett*

Originally those Arches were just holes in the cliff; with their half boats up against the wall. They had what they call 'rope houses' on the beach where they stored their nets. The Council offered to build these Arches at a peppercorn rent, forever, if they'd take the rope houses off the beach because Brighton was so popular as a holiday resort. Which they did, but now they've driven them from the beach, and the Corporation want to charge thousands of pounds a year for them.

*Joe Mitchell*

*The bandstand on the seafront at Hove in 1976*

The day started as a good day. I was almost at my seventeenth birthday and going to change my mode of transport as a present to myself. I set out from Whitehawk on my Suzuki motorbike to ride along the front to Beamish's on the coast road near Shoreham, where I had arranged to pick up my new bike. As I rode along Madeira Drive there were a lot of young people in jeans and leather jackets who waved and cheered as I passed by. A bit bemused by this I was again surprised as, passing the Palace Pier, a group of lads in parkas jumped out at me, cursing and throwing things. I accelerated and felt something hit my crash helmet.

Once I'd picked up my new bike, a Lambretta scooter, I returned the same way with very different reactions. This time the mods were all smiles and waves while the rockers threw things. I hadn't changed, but all they saw was the bike.

*A Mod in August 1978*

*A rockabilly in 1982*

At the time in Brighton I'm not sure we had the same rivalry as was obvious in those first seaside battles. The boys who lived out in the country tended to ride motorbikes, dress in leathers and like rock music. In the town, the boys tended towards smart Italian suits, cut slim with ultra-narrow lapels and they enjoyed Ska and Blue Beat. The groups stayed separate and attended different pubs and clubs. They avoided each other and trouble was rare. Or perhaps I was just a very naïve teenager!

*Barry Silsby*

During my student days in Brighton - 1969-73 - the sea and seafront went mostly unacknowledged; the territory of holiday makers and day trippers. Although of course the pebbly beach was the place for midnight swimming and musings on the meaning of life as well as memorable moments such as sitting in a beached rowing boat, eating Russian Salad straight from its polystyrene pot.

My first student accommodation was in Lower Rock Gardens; a small, shared room right at the top of the house with a wonderful roof-scape and no space whatsoever for studying. There was a small 'sitting room' in the basement, which was really the living space for the host family but was the only place we were allowed to have visitors. The owners were obliged to provide us with B&B plus weekend meals.

In the winter, we all discovered the problems of living in summer holiday rooms let as 'all-year' accommodation. There was no heating in the rooms at all until, after much protesting on both sides, we were provided with portable electrical heaters. Whatever else we learned in our studies, we all acquired a good understanding of how many old shillings it took to heat a room to a just-tolerable 16°C.

*Sue Yearley*

Leslie Whitcomb

*The Concorde Club and the Palace Pier in January 1982*

GRAND

Leslie Whitcomb

**WE TOOK MARGARET THATCHER OUT**, the Prime Minister, although she was Leader of the Opposition at the time. I took her out in 1975. I advised her not to go because it was a little bit choppy. It was arranged that she came down to visit our club and we wanted obviously to get our spoke in about the Common Market, the fishing side, not because of the boating, because of the limits. I advised against going this day because we wouldn't have took ordinary passengers out, it was a little bit just on the borderline. And she was very insistent to go, to be seen to be in a boat, as her predecessor Edward Heath, used to be a sailor.

I went and got the boat, and it just seemed to lay calm for a little bit, so I shouted to her, 'Come on,' I don't think I actually said, 'Cock your leg up and get in here,' but, 'Come on, jump in here if you want to go,' a bit quick. And we took her out for an half hour's spin round the Piers, she got wringing wet, the photographers obviously all wanted a picture of her being wringing wet.

*Alan Hayes* Catching Stories

Glenn Stevens

*The Grand Hotel re-opening after the bombing in late 1984*

The IRA bombing of the Grand Hotel on 12 October 1984 is well recorded, but there is a little-known aspect of the following day's conference. When the bomb went off wrecking the hotel, killing five people and injuring 34, Mrs Thatcher was taken to Sussex Police HQ, Lewes. The hotel was in chaos and those that were not injured were taken away quickly, many covered in debris. A Marks & Spencer director was at the hotel, who contacted Head Office to get M&S Brighton open in top secret with just the manager and the senior warehouseman. I was working for M&S at the time and saw the photos that were taken in the store that night. The entire Tory cabinet were taken there for a complete clothes refit. I saw the image of Sir Keith Joseph having his inside leg measured! So that at 9.30 next morning all appeared bandbox new on the platform.

*Geoffrey Mead*

Brighton had a very lively campaign group opposed to the 1988 law, Section 28, brought in by Thatcher's government to forbid the "promotion of homosexuality" by local councils, and it spoke of lesbian and gay relationships as being "pretended families". So, in 1990 when we heard that an evangelical Christian group which promoted a narrow view of "family values" was coming to the Brighton Centre, we decided to take action. Even better, Princess Diana was to be the keynote speaker...

On the day of the event, as a noisy demo took place outside the venue, five activists, disguised as normal people, entered the conference. They sat quietly as the first speakers came and went, but when Princess Diana took to the platform, they silently mounted the stage and stood in a line behind her, holding placards proclaiming "Lesbian mothers are not pretending", stood for a moment, placed the placards on the table and filed off the stage, to be ejected by security back to the jubilant crowd of protesters on the sea front.

Needless to say this hit the front-page headlines, "BLUSHING DI IN GAY GIRLS' DEMO SCARE" proclaimed one tabloid somewhat hyperbolically. Strangely, the Family Congress never returned to Brighton. And what Princess Di thought will never be known, but we suspected she would have been with us.

*Melita Dennett*

Peter Chrisp

I walked past her [the West Pier] once with the family while the film "Oh What a Lovely War" was being made. The pier was closed to the public so we did not stop. In 1970 the southern end of the pier was closed to the public, followed by complete closure in 1979. I often drove past her noticing the further damage and neglect.

When the hurricane struck I thought it would be her [the West Pier] end, but her strong heart and the genius of her designer and builder Eugenius Birch saw her through. Her condition worsened and I, along with the majority of Brighton and Hove residents, was guilty of that neglect through indifference.

*Dave Huggins*

The story of Club Shame starts as far back as 1980. In those politically fraught times, with Margaret Thatcher at the country's helm and homophobia all around, I ran a club called Subterfuge in a small basement venue at the Apollo Hotel on the seafront.

Subterfuge was billed as 'alternative'; it was a melting pot of youth cultures and boasted a hugely diverse crowd of punks, skinheads, Goths, rockabillies, students, drag queens, new romantics, arty types and everything in between, all crowding the dance floor and all sharing some kind of common value despite their differing 'tribes'. It had an exciting, dangerous and dynamic atmosphere.

The Zap Club, when it opened in 1984 in its arch under King's Road, seemed dazzling and original, but in many ways was just another in a long line of moments when the sea came to the rescue of the town. Whatever its claims to novelty at the time, and, make no mistake, it was indeed daring and singular at its birth, it was one marker in a long history.

*Paul Kemp* Zap, Twenty-five years of innovation

I came to Brighton in 1986. There were a lot more public toilets back then, and a lot fewer venues in which to meet like-minded men. All of the conveniences along the seafront from the Angel of Peace to the Bushes were cottages. I used to walk a circuit of all the seafront toilets, in the hope of meeting other gentlemen like myself. There was one sweet old queen, in his late 60s or early 70s, doing the same thing as me, and he took to saying as we passed each other "Once more round the esplanade dear?"

*A seafront toilet known as 'a cottage'*

The decaying arches under the west pier were also a hot bed of action. I was in there one night, right at the back with a local hairdresser, a real Brighton character that everyone knew. Then I saw torches in the darkness: it was the police coming in. The hairdresser zipped up really quickly and I got up and pulled my trousers up too. It was very busy in there, lots of men, so I thought I could get away with it if I slipped out through some panels at the back. I had just put my head through when I saw two police men looking at me. "Good evening sir, what brings you here tonight?" I explained that I had been caught short and had nipped in to relieve myself, however there now seemed to be a bit of a situation... I'm not sure if they believed me or not but they told me to go, and go quickly.

I think this was 1993. The arches were boarded up after that, spoiling our fun.

*Piers*

In the 1980s the Metropole Hotel hosted arms fairs which were enthusiastically picketed by anti-war protesters held back by barricades and heavy policing.

At the 1992 Tory Party conference at the Brighton Centre I was part of a large National Union of Students protest against student loans. We marched from The Level to the Brighton Centre and assembled on the seafront opposite the venue. I carried a large black bazooka which a friend had made from a drainpipe for a play about the IRA, with the words "Bang Goes Education" painted down the side, and decided to complete the look with a black beret and sunglasses.

As our noisy demo chanted against the government of John Major, I glanced up at the roof of the Brighton Centre to see what looked remarkably like sniper rifles trained on us. You wouldn't get away with carrying a fake bazooka on a demo now – you'd be arrested, or even shot!

*Melita Dennett*

On July 13 2002 the first Fat Boy Slim beach party was held; at the time, I was a tour guide on the West Pier and was asked by the manager if I was available for some night work. It transpired that the Big Beach Boutique event was to have a massive firework display and that the West Pier was to be the launch area.

All that afternoon a swarm of workmen descended on the pier with miles of cabling and colossal boxes of fireworks. The long hot afternoon drew in the crowds and by sunset the beach was invisible with people and the sea was covered in every conceivable floating object. Not being a 'clubber', the music was completely new to me but of course immensely infectious! At the end of the concert the fireworks were electronically ignited and the effect was amazing with the summer night sky lit up and the reflections from the water.

*Geoffrey Mead*

I was a guide on the West Pier in 2002 when it was a romantic ruin. We could only take groups out as far as the concert hall as the end of the pier with the theatre was unsafe at the time.

If it was a fairly stormy day the first guide on duty would go to the end of the walkway to see if it was safe. If we returned unbattered by the winds and still standing upright all would go ahead. The groups actually liked the stormy weather – more exciting! So too was the wearing of life jackets and hard hats.

Entering the abandoned concert hall, with its broken windows, peeling paint and delicious decaying atmosphere was particularly wonderful. Ghosts of the past swirled around and one could almost hear the music of the bands that once played there. The smell of guano (pigeon excrement) was pungent and it was the men who would almost faint from the noxious aroma.

*Sarah Tobias*

*A demonstrator outside the Brighton Centre in October 1980*

61

Club Barracuda at 139 King's Road Arches was home to The Perfume Garden for a year at the start of the new millennium. It described itself as "Monthly hard clubbing for gay men, lesbians and their special friends." The width of a single arch, it was rammed with sweaty over-excited clubbers (no air-con) and possibly no licence (you bought drinks with raffle tickets). In the early hours, spangly clubbers could be seen wandering out to sit on the beach, slowly coming down as the sun came up.

It was never going to last forever. The loved-up polysexual clubbers had to move to a more stable (legal?) venue, and it settled at Pool/Envy above Charles Street. It had monthly themes, elaborate decorations, and stunning lasers.

On Friday 23 March 2003, the club was celebrating co-founder Kitty's birthday. Nick March and Superfast Oz kept the BPM high and 'Perfect' Pete Bennett (later to win Big Brother 7) was raving in the crowd with everyone else. After the club finished at 2am, a crowd of happy clubbers headed down to the beach but were met with a not so happy sight.

Smoke was billowing out from the grade 1 listed West Pier. It had been weather-damaged in the winter storms and was now a sorry sight. The fire had been raging most of Friday and was still smouldering with small fires visible in the darkness. An eerie sight on my walk home to Hove, I sat with many others and pondered its demise. This was most definitely not the Café del Mar vibe of old.

*Alf Le Flohic*

JJ Waller

*The West Pier burning, 2003*

Back in 2003 I was studying film at Northbrook College and spending the day with fellow students, wandering around Brighton with an old 16mm Bolex camera. Whilst aimlessly taking street footage, one of our group heard on his portable radio about a fire at the West Pier so we immediately ran down to the beach to find it ablaze.

I had only moved to Sussex from Bristol less than a year prior, so had few personal memories of the West Pier, and knew very little about its grand history. However, I could tell that what confronted us as we arrived at the beach was a very significant and sad moment for Brighton and Hove. It was a strange and awful sight. The flames were so all-consuming we were expecting the whole structure to completely give way at any moment. People on the beach were already gossiping about how it could have happened; "a cigarette", "arson", "I'm sure I saw a boat speed away just before the flames".

The only thing I really gave any thought to at that moment was how best to document what I was seeing. I took wide angle footage of the pier burning, the birds and helicopters circling overhead, onlookers taking photographs, and some close-ups of the police tape that had been placed around the end of the pier. Eventually my film roll ran out.

Once the footage had been developed we projected it onto a wall back at the college. Being old 16mm film stock it looked like something out of the 1950s and had a fittingly elegiac and nostalgic quality.

*James Tucker*

Nowadays I am a supervisor in the Brighton Thistle Hotel where I have been working for fourteen years. Over those years I have seen a lot of famous people as well as holiday makers. I have seen political figures, such as Neil Kinnock, John Smith and Tony Blair, sports legends, like the South African and Indian cricket teams, Steffi Graf and many others. The wedding of Chris Eubank was held in the hotel and the boxing promoter Don King and lots of American boxers were also there. I have seen many pop stars, movie stars and TV soap stars.

Working life has its ups and downs just like the British weather. The view of the seafront with all the holiday makers looks amazing. Unfortunately, it gets so busy in the hotel that we can't enjoy our city's popularity and activities as much as others can.

My favourite pastime in this seaside city is fishing. We go by boat from the Marina and we catch mostly mackerel and sea bass. The fish are greatly appreciated at family barbeques in the summer.

All in all, living in Brighton is wonderful and I wouldn't move from here for anything in the world

*Unattributed* Bangla Brighton

*Brighton Pier, 2011*

*Looking west from the Brighton Wheel in 2011*

I arrived in Brighton with just one bag and, for the first few days, I had no bed and lived in the cellar of someone's house. Eventually I found somewhere to live and now I have my own room.

Living here is very expensive. I can't afford to eat out, so I do all my own cooking. I cook Turkish food with lots of vegetables. I also can't afford to use public transport and I walk everywhere.Anonymous – *Refuge* I particularly enjoy being on the seafront and walking by the sea.

*Anonymous* Refuge

An estimated 100,000 Brighton & Hove Albion fans lined the seafront route from Madeira Drive to Hove Lawns to celebrate our heroes' dramatic ascent to the Premier League. This was too big for me, a lifelong Albion fan, to miss out on. I was so happy, pleased and proud that my beloved Albion had made it to the top division.

Amidst all the excitement of knowing the city would be having yet another fabulous celebration, the hot May sunshine beating down on us made for a perfect day.

The bus parade took an hour longer than expected, such was the feeling of joy and elation which we all wanted to share. Everyone took in the party atmosphere from start to finish. The players finally arrived at Hove Lawns with the rose glow of the late afternoon sunshine perfectly colouring the emotional, noisy, carnival-like scenes and, with the sun in our eyes, we welcomed our heroes onstage.

*Alan Wares*

*The West Pier in 2011*

When I was a schoolboy in the 1920's we lived in Powys Square, opposite St. Michael's Church. I've travelled all over the world since then. When I returned, some years ago, I was devastated to see my beloved West Pier almost in ruins. I immediately joined the West Pier Trust. I must say that I was quite excited by the i360 project. Maybe I could see my old happy hunting ground from on high. Imagine my delight when I was invited to make a celebratory trip ("flight") on my 100th birthday in 2016. Would I be able to see Powys Square and the church from the top of the tower?

I entered the gate with my whole family. I was interviewed about the 'West Pier in my day' by a TV reporter, who announced to the public that it was my birthday, and the whole 200 sang "Happy Birthday to You".

The ascent was so slow one hardly noticed it. At the top I leaned on the rail and peered northwards. Sure enough, there was the church and, beside it, Powys Square. I could also just make out St. Anne's Well Gardens, the scene of my primitive attempts at cricket and football. I drank in all the other familiar areas as we descended and there, at the bottom, I looked at the Grand and the Metropole whose facades, in the old days, suggested impossible bastions of privilege.

I had been able to renew my acquaintance with the old familiar area of my youth. What a thrill!

*Len Goldman*

# Contributors

**Melita Dennett** moved to Hove in 1986 in search of adventure and continues to find it daily.

**Dave Huggins** was born in Brighton, lived most of his 82 years in Hove and most importantly by the seaside. The extracts are taken from his autobiography.

**Alf Le Flohic** - 'I arrived in the summer in 1987, just in time to watch from my room as the Great Storm took out the lights across town. I'd never lived in a place with such a sense of drama. I wasn't going anywhere.'

**Peter James** is the author of the international bestselling Roy Grace novels, published in 37 languages, with over 19m copies sold. Born and raised in Brighton, he has homes in London and in Sussex, the latter which he and his wife, Lara, share with three dogs and an assortment of alpacas, emus, ducks and hens.

**Geoffrey Mead** is a Brighton 'native' who teaches geography at the University of Sussex, with a long research interest in the coastal strip of the city, both its physical and human landscapes, and especially its resort and piers' histories.

**Barry Silsby** was born 'up the grubber' - Brighton General Hospital, previously Brighton Workhouse - and went to Whitehawk Infant and Junior Schools and Westlain Grammar (now BACA). Leaving Brighton to attend college he returned to the Brighton area 18 years ago.

**Sarah Tobias** is a lecturer in social, cultural and local history, Sussex University tutor, tour guide and writer. Originally from London, she has lived in Brighton for many years.

**James Tucker** is a video maker who grew up in Bristol, but like many before him, ran away to Brighton. He loves cinema, ideas, coffee and lens flares.

**Alan Wares** is a rarity in Brighton - he was born here. He supports Brighton & Hove Albion, public transport and loves the city - making the Albion Bus Parade along the seafront one of the most memorable days of his life.

**Piers** - 'I first came to Brighton in 1979 as a student, came back in 1986 for a dirty weekend, and never left...'

JJ Waller

*The i360 in 2017*

# Books

Extracts for this compilation were taken from the following QueenSpark books:

**At the Pawnbrokers** - This 1991 memoir by Lillie Morgan tells an often shocking story of the grinding poverty faced by working people in Brighton during the First World War.

**Hard Times and Easy Terms** - This is the entertaining story of a young cockney, who was something of a 'wide boy'. Originally from London, Bert Healey's story begins with tales of his life as a wayward boy in Brighton during the First World War. He also describes many aspects of his working life – from his first pay packet, when working as a taxi driver to his times of unemployment during times of illness.

**Shops Book** - This 1978 book is about shopkeepers and street traders, based on interviews with people whose families had been trading in Brighton for decades. These vivid memories tell stories of hardship, determination, camaraderie, and enterprise.

**The Town Beehive** – This book was first published in 1975 and was so popular that it quickly sold out. Brightonian Daisy Noakes tells her story from the age of fourteen, when she went into service. She gives us an insight into the life of a woman born and brought up in Brighton.

**The Church Round the Corner** – Maurice Packham examines the social and religious history of St. Anne's Church, which was located in the heart of Brighton. Maurice was a choirboy at St. Anne's in the 1930s, and he takes a humorous look at the community of his fellow worshippers.

**A Pen for All Seasons** - Published in 1997, this anthology is the outcome of work that was produced by members of the Hove Writers Club. Including poetry and prose, it focuses on the details of everyday life through the medium of creative writing.

**Catching Stories** - This 1996 account of the fishing industry documents how it has changed since the beginning of the 20th century. At that time, fishing boats landed on the beach and the fish market was actually on the seafront. On a more personal level, Catching Stories is a living record, told in their own words, of the individuals who made up Brighton's fishing community.

**A Working Man** - One winter in the 1980s, Ernie Mason was at a loose end, so he bought a notebook and began to write his autobiography. This story encapsulates a working-class man's journey through life over the course of the twentieth century, documenting the many changes that took place in the local environment and in social conditions.

**The Smiling Bakers** - In his 1992 memoir, George Grout recalled the years when he lived and worked at the well-known family bakery at 34 Coombe Road.

**A Life Behind Bars** - Born in 1908 at the Marquess of Exeter public house (now the Chimney House), which was run by her parents, Marjory Batchelor spent her working life as a barmaid and pub landlady in and around the Brighton area. Marjory recalls her experiences of two World Wars and beyond in Brighton, Worthing, Rottingdean, Mile Oak and Portsmouth.

**Boxing Day Baby** - Barbara Chapman was born in Brighton on a snowy Boxing Day in 1927. In this 1994 autobiography, she reminisces about her early childhood; focusing on her memories of home and school, and the effects of the WWII on herself, her family, and the community.

**Moulsecoomb Days** - In her 1990 autobiography, Ruby Dunn recalls the development of Moulsecoomb, then a rural outskirt of Brighton, into a post-World War One "garden suburb".

**The Circle of Life** - This is Olive Masterson's tale of growing up in the Richmond Road area of Brighton between the Wars. She recounts the trials and tribulations of an ordinary hardworking Brightonian woman, who dealt stoically with the many problems she faced in her life, including diphtheria in the family and the ill-health of her father, who was the principal wage-earner.

**Back Street Brighton** - Originally produced in collaboration with the Lewis Cohen Urban Studies Centre, this book incorporates photographs taken by the Environmental Health Department in the late forties and early fifties of houses in Brighton that were scheduled for demolition in the fifties and sixties. Each photograph is accompanied by reminiscences of families who lived in the houses.

**Everything Seems Smaller** - Sid Manville reminisces about his Brighton boyhood between the wars. This first-person account of growing up in Bear Road, which was effectively his playground, describes scenes where he and his friends rolled their hoops and played with their spinning tops.

**International Service** - With its backdrop of Brighton in the Second World War, International Service tells the tale of Kathleen Wilson's naive teenage years, leaving school at 14 on the outbreak of war to work in a factory, going on to work in a baker's, as a domestic help and in the grocery trade.

**Brighton Behind the Front** - First published in 1990, Brighton Behind the Front brings together a collection of Brighton World War Two reminiscences and documents how ordinary people were affected by the war.

**Brighton Boy** - This 1994 memoir is a schoolboy's tale of Brighton in the 1950s, seen through the eyes of Andy Steer. He recalls Brighton characters and shops, swimming at Black Rock and with the "Shiverers" Swimming Club at the salt-water King Alfred pool in Hove.

**School Reports** - This book contains reminiscences and anecdotes from past pupils who attended St. Luke's School, in the Queens Park area of Brighton in the years between 1908 – 1983.

**Oh! What a Lovely Pier** - Working on the West Pier from 1956 to 1970, Daphne Mitchell's 1996 memoir evokes the atmosphere of the seaside in bygone times. Daphne recalls seaside shows that featured acts such as local stunt man the Great Omani, floating by on a bed of nails.

**Daring Hearts** - This is the definitive guide to queer life in Brighton in the 1950s and 60s. It's made up of a searing and informative collection of life stories based on taped interviews with forty lesbians and gay men who spoke openly about their lives in and around Brighton. Originally published in collaboration with Brighton Ourstory.

**Snapshots** - In her 1996 autobiography, Janis Ravenett recalls her memories of growing up in Southampton Street in the Hanover area of Brighton, during the years between 1942 and 1955.

**I Do Like To Be Beside The Seaside** - This selection of creative writing is the cumulative work of fifty people, who attended a writing weekend in Seaford, East Sussex in July 1993.

**Deckhand, West Pier** - Arthur Thickett's 1993 memoir is the story of a young man who came to Brighton in the summer of 1970, full of hope and optimism – his goal was to find adventure and ultimately love. On his first day he found digs in Ovingdean, on his second day he walked into a job as a deckhand on the West Pier.

**The Crowd Roars** - In his 1998 memoir Ron Cunningham, alias 'The Great Omani', presents tales and adventures from the life of a professional stuntman.

**Zap, Twenty Five Years of Innovation** – Published in 2006 this book uses the Zap Art's collection of videos, posters, flyers, listings, recordings and other artefacts to chart the organisation's wild ride across a diverse cultural terrain encompassing groundbreaking club nights, performers, poets, musicians, dancers, comedians, Live Artists, DJs and pyrotechnicians.

**Bangla Brighton** - Poetic and passionate, lively and lyrical, Bangla Brighton is a series of moving true accounts of life on the South coast by Brighton and Hove's Bangladeshi community.

**Refuge** - The Migrant English Project at The Cowley Club offered language classes to newly arrived migrants to Brighton and Hove. This book is the result of a series of workshops where participants had the opportunity to tell their stories.

**Roofless** – This book is a collection of photographs, essays, stories and poems by homeless and ex-homeless people from Brighton. There is anger, sadness and rebellion, but also instances of hope and solidarity and writing that, whilst often raw and uncompromising, possesses a surprising generosity of spirit.

# Acknowledgements

**Volunteer reading group**

Kerry Boettcher, Melita Dennett, Esther Gill, Gerry Holloway, Geoffrey Mead, Charlotte Overton-Hart, Catherine Page, Jo Palache, John Riches, Barry Silsby and Sarah Tobias.

**Project Managers**

John Riches and Melita Dennett

QueenSpark Books would like to thank all of the authors and contributors who have kindly given us their stories. We would particularly like to thank Len Goldman for the use of extracts from his own memoir - Oh What a Lovely Shore (Brighton in the Twenties Through the Eyes of a Schoolboy) - and his account of his 100th birthday.

'Thanks also to those who generously donated their photographs to our website, www.photosbrightonandhove.org.uk

Nigel Bailey, Mary Belton, Margaret Boniface, Peter Chrisp, G Curran, David Fisher, Christopher Frewin, Esther Georgiles, Herb Goulden, Ned Hoskins, Joan Landen, Charlotte Leaper, Allan Marriott, Maureen Middlemiss, Barry Pitman, David Sewell, Glenn Stevens, JJ Waller and Peter Whitcomb (on behalf of his late father, Leslie).

For allowing us to use photographs from their collection (including the cover), we thank the Royal Pavilion & Museums, Brighton & Hove, and particularly Kevin Bacon for his assistance.

# Kickstarter Supporters

Prue Baker, Zoe Barton, Caraline Brown, Eamonn Burke-Duggan, Sheila Clarke, Simon Cross, Stephen Darby, Nicola Demott, Melita Dennett, Gerry Hussein, Margaretta Jolly, Rog Newman, Barry Pitman, Dan Robertson, Dorothy Sheridan and Andy Silsby.

Barry Pitman

*The Cliffhanger Theatre group performing in front of the Athina B in February 1980*